Matt Bird lives in Provo, Utah, near his childhood home. He is currently studying at Brigham Young University. He wrote *He Atoned for Me* while serving a two-year volunteer mission in Montana and Wyoming. Matt's father, Brian Bird, was a well-known artist in the community. His father's religious artworks helped inspire many of the works found within *He Atoned for Me*, including the poem titled "My Father the Sculptor."

To Dad

To Maddy

Matt Bird

HE ATONED FOR ME

AUSTIN MACAULEY PUBLISHERS™

LONDON · CAMBRIDGE · NEW YORK · SHARJAH

Ordering Information:
Quantity sales: special discounts are available on quantity purchases by corporations, associations, and others. For details, contact the publisher at the address below.

Publisher's Cataloging-in-Publication data
Bird, Matt
He Atoned for Me

ISBN 9781643785479 (Paperback)
ISBN 9781643785486 (Hardback)
ISBN 9781645368144 (ePub e-book)

Library of Congress Control Number: 2019914096

The main category of the book — POETRY / Subjects & Themes / Inspirational & Religious

www.austinmacauley.com/us

First Published (2019)
Austin Macauley Publishers LLC
40 Wall Street, 28th Floor
New York, NY 10005
USA

mail-usa@austinmacauley.com
+1 (646) 5125767

I would like to give credit for this work to the Savior. He is the one these poems are pointing to. They are about His Gospel. Without Him, this would not have been possible.

He Atoned for Me

How great the love of my savior,
He atoned for me.

However could I repay Him,
but with a broken heart.

My soul contrite forced to my knees,
I plead unto my Father.

Let my misdeeds be forgotten,
let my Lord's pain be no more in vain.

This day I give my sins to Thee,
this guilt upon my shoulders.

Oh, the pain, the grief,
the suffering, of that great Jehovah.

Was mine the one to make Him bend,
to make Him bleed, to make Him suffer?

Was I the one to force a crown of thorns upon His head?

Was mine the one to burst His veins,
to fill His pours with blood?

Was I the one to make a cup so bitter for Him to drink?

Was mine the one to cause all this?
Oh Lord was it I?

Of course it was, I am but a man,
I'm weak, I'm small, I'm mortal.

Oh, how I wish to drink the dregs,
to make the plea, to take His place in suffering.

But I am weak, and He is strong,
He is the One Begotten.

I accept my role, I know my place,
I will not waste what He freely gave.

For I shall be betrayed,
ambushed, berated.

By that which gives me life,
by that which Adam gained.

But mercy prevails for I soon will see,
my Lord and my Redeemer.

The greatest who ever lived,
He bled, He died, for me.

I am the one to burst His veins,
filling His pours with blood.

Without my sin, would he have suffered,
perhaps a little less?

I love my God, yet I still sin,
I continue in my ways.

Do I hurt Him more,
each time that I do wrong?

This thought is false,
the debt is fully paid.

His love goes past what I can see,
He suffered so I could live.

Because of His undying grace,
I know I may be redeemed.

If I but live as he has asked,
from hell I am preserved.

He is the one true God's begotten,
He atoned for me.

Stones and Arrows

I stand upon this wall,
the fear of God has brought me here.

Preaching to those who would not hear,
yet still I must contend.

The words of God flow through my mouth,
to pierce the heart of all those who doubt.

The son of man soon shall come,
prepare your minds and hearts.

Do no more evil,
come unto God,
and receive eternal life!

Rejoice in Him who will surely come,
repent and be baptized!

The ears of men cannot hear these words,
for they are filled with pride.

Anger fills their hearts,
for all they hear,
are the devil's deceiving lies.

No stone or arrow pierces my skin,
in righteousness do I strive.

My Father's spirit fills my soul,
I am a son of God.

For I am Samuel the Lamanite,
and the Lord sent I.

A Day, a Night, and a Day

The day set,
the time departing.

Where must our savior be?
For death becomes those that believe.

I call upon the One to come,
He answers graciously.

"I come upon the morrow,
do not let your strife complete."

"Have faith in me,
hold back your fears."

"Have courage,
strength, belief."

The sun is gone,
yet the day remains.

The son of God has come at last,
to save our souls from sorrow.

Betraying minds fill with grief,
and lay down in the dust.

Conversion spreads on this great day,
of those who won't believe.

My brother now is born this day,
I also am a son of God.

I am Nephi, a special witness, the Lord has come this day!

Blessed Among Women

I have been chosen and blessed by God,
to do his will,
to be his hands.

The Holy Ghost will come upon me,
I will bear the son of God.

I will bring my savior into this world,
to raise Him in His glory.

To grieve the loss,
to praise our God,
to find Him preaching truth.

To give the world what it sorely needs,
this night in Bethlehem.

The shepherds come,
wise men proclaim.

A wicked man begins to slay,
for fear has gripped his heart.

The One Begotten will not be found,
the One who will atone.

I have given the Savior life,
I am blessed and I am chosen.

I am the Virgin Mary,
the mother of our God.

The Soldier

I pull a man on a leash,
as I have many others.

I know not of his speech,
nor of his country.

Rome is my nation,
I believe not of the Jews.

My master has spoken,
and I must obey.

A wicked man released,
a righteous one imprisoned.

I watch as He is printed,
stripes grow across His back.

The whip slices deeper through,
I look into His eyes.

In replace of self-pity, pain, and grief,
Is strength, light and triumph!

Scarlet tossed upon His shoulders,
a crown placed on His head.

A king He is called,
as an imposter He is treated.

I push Him forward to His death,
the weapon upon His back.

The courage in His step,
the vitality of His burden.

I pound into his hands,
I pound into his feet.

I have obeyed the command,
I have crucified this man.

Love is in his eyes,
my heart begins to burn.

Forgiveness in the words He speaks,
my soul is filled with grief.

He cries unto the heavens,
forsaken has He been.

He leaves his body upon this tree,
and ascends back to His Father.

Guilt and sorrow rest upon my soldiers,
as darkness engulfs the land.

This Roman soldier now believes,
the one true son of God!

The Living Witness

My eyes are opened,
the vapor rising.

Mountains raised where valleys claimed,
cities fallen as the wicked souls.

Piercing voices, cleansing minds.
Our God descending, from on high.

I come to feel the holes and scars,
of that Redeemer who is mine.

I fall to Earth from whence I came,
to worship Him who came this day.

"Become as children to be saved,
no man may dwell with me."

"Have no fault,
take up My name."

"Judge not the man who does you wrong,
for justice is none but mine."

"The ten lost men have faith alike,
for them I too must save."

"Moses has died and gone away,
this law now ye shall keep."

"Eat My body, drink My blood,
and always remember Me."

Twelve men He calls,
I hear my name.

I dare not ask what I desire,
to bring all men to His great fire.

Yet He knows all,
and comes to me.

Now I am His disciple,
and I am here to this day.

My Father the Sculptor

My Father is a sculptor,
His workshop I am in.

I am hard, I am cold,
I have lost my form.

Yet in the hands of the Master,
if I let Him do His work.

In His hands I will soften,
with His warmth I cannot falter.

His thumb will clear my streaks,
will smooth my imperfections.

His fingers make no error,
His tools create perfection.

He will form me,
from a man I should not be.

Mold me,
into what he sees inside.

Change me,
when I give my life for Him.

He will reclaim me from the darkness,
carve me from a marble frame.

For then and only then,
will I last forever.

My heart once hard, once cold,
once broken.

Will be finally complete,
In Him who has not forgotten.

I will rely on Him, the Master,
the sculptor!

It Shall Be Given Him

Seek and ye shall find,
knock and it shall be opened unto you.

Ask and you shall receive,
receive and sin no longer.

Ask not what thou seek not,
seek not what thou fearest.

Your time cannot be wasted,
serve with all your might.

Sow no misery,
reap no pain.

The last day soon shall come,
accept your Lord and Savior.

Do not die this day,
do not simply remain.

Wallow not in all thy torment,
fear and pain.

Unquenchable shall be the fire,
eternity shall it burn.

For those who listen not,
and fall into the tempter's snare.

Thy vile and thy gnashers of teeth,
wail not wile thou hast a chance.

Return to Him whom gave thee life,
let not your heart rebel.

Find where your heart resides,
pick your side and live.

For what man seeketh he shall find,
and it shall be given him.

Waiting for You

Guilt resides inside my heart,
refusing to relieve.

I cannot turn away,
I cannot forget the pain.

I turn to the One,
I was taught would save.

I return to the ground,
the dirt from where I came.

My proud heart down onto the dust,
below what God commands.

One word I whisper from my mouth,
before I'm forced to stop.

Love seeps into my broken heart,
fire cleanses my rage-filled soul.

Being lifted from the depths,
a pit without an end.

Embraced in my savior's arms,
I receive what I did seek.

He whispers in a still small voice:
"I have been waiting for you to speak."

Stripling Warrior

Weapons buried,
a covenant made.

The battle raging,
masters are claimed.

Bodies tarnished,
yet God is praised.

The young enlist,
to serve their Lord.

Though danger nigh,
their courage takes.

They fly from home,
from their mothers' care.

To join the battle,
to win and heir.

Though bruised and battered,
cut and bleeding.

Though broken, injured,
none complain.

Our savior's work continues on,
we must be bold and strong.

We are the stripling warriors of our day,
called to serve and fight.

We will be torn,
and tempted to stray.

Yet prepared are we,
to fight the fight.

Our mothers taught,
the true right way.

We will be triumphant,
come what may.

For I am a soldier,
enlisted to fight.

In my savior's ranks,
prepared for today.

Sent by the Lord,
to teach and save.

A Serpent of Brass

Fiery serpents fly through the land,
at Israel's wicked hand.

For the wicked they come,
they who murmur and strife.

The fire is subtle,
as the death which it brings.

Death will preside,
to those who give in.

Stubborn at heart,
you submit to the pain.

Deliver us from death,
which our bitterness caused.

They cry to a man who once split the sea,
who once made them free.

A serpent was raised,
as an answer from God.

Of brass was it made,
to heal all in pain.

This fire will bite,
yet not all must die.

Look upon God,
for his answer was made.

Show faith and you'll live,
you will be saved from this fate.

The fire will bite,
and the brass will protect.

The fire will fight,
yet the fire will die.

The fire will bite,
though the brass will remain.

Follow Him made of brass,
and you will be saved.

My Eternal God

No longer my head turned from Thee,
I am searching for the fold.

Accept and return me,
help me to find Thee, oh Lord.

My God,
my Father

I fell from thy mercy,
lift this burden with me.

Show me to the path,
I have lost my way.

Thou Redeemer of my soul,
thy grace upon my spirit.

Thou hast succored me,
Thou hast raised me up.

The bread of life I search for,
the living water do I seek.

Give me all Thou has to give,
show me all that I can be.

Fallen

Once great now forgotten.

An angel falls through the clouds.

His heart once pure, now deranged.

Our brother, and our friend, cannot see the light.

Never to rise, never to conquer, always to fall, always to fail.

Misery brings malice to his heart, and a smile to his face.

Mammon knows no joy, Satan has no hope.

Lucifer, once a light, is now a dead and rising smoke.

I was meant to conquer, I was sent to fight.

I will show no fear, I will stand my ground.

I will prevail, I will endure unto the end.

I will not fall as he once did.

Starry Night

I look deep into the midst of the universe,
stars clinging to the sky.

A mist of whirlwind swirling,
a vast darkness before me.

Warmth wraps around my heart,
I realize with humility.

This glorious view travels,
simply for the pleasure of my eyes.

I now understand the question,
I have been seeking just beyond my grasp.

All I need now do is reach,
Through a veil of darkness.

A shadow that stands in my way,
blocking a hidden path before me.

I follow the whisper of hope,
into the unknown.

A glimpse of fear,
that I am simply speaking to myself.

Quickly it dissipates,
clarity fills my heart and mind.

I feel my God embrace my very soul,
I now know that this is my Redeemer.

And to think all I need do,
was ask.

Among the Roses

I search among the roses,
yet each has frayed and browned.

I cannot find what I am searching for,
perhaps it is too late.

There must be more,
I know that there is.

A perfect rose,
just waiting to be found.

I can glimpse the beauty in my mind,
vivid colors and the sweetest smell.

I search and search but cannot find,
that rose that I desire.

I return to my most desperate state,
and I plead with the gardener.

He speaks to me with loving care,
and shows me to the path.

He hands me the smallest seed,
and tells me it will grow.

Find the richest soil,
the choicest ground.

A perfect rose will bloom and grow,
and it will never die.

Good Samaritan

I try to walk a narrow path,
right down the road I need.

My destination far yet to go,
but still I journey on.

At first, I feel I know my way,
but others try to sway.

I know not who I can trust,
or who is in my way.

A gentle voice then leads me on,
to where I need to go.

I walk the bold and narrow path,
somehow I have lost.

It runs straight through winding roads,
that lead to eternal doom.

I find the end of an iron rod,
I quickly grab a hold.

I walk on with ease,
with this anchor in my hand.

I listen and I hear the voice,
that calls to all the world.

"Come unto me and find your life,
for all eternity."

I know the voice, I remember not,
where I heard it once.

I fight on through the mist and fog,
holding tight to the rod.

The smoke then clears, and I can see,
my final destination.

I make it there and reach to partake,
but someone stops me there.

"You are not done, you still have work,
go back and do for others what I have done for you."

I Am Not Alone

I know I am not alone,
I feel a helping hand.

I know that I must go,
God has called me to His land.

I find that I can scarcely walk,
this trail of blood and tears.

But yet I feel a guiding force,
which helps me move away my fears.

I leave a trail behind me,
my feet now torn and frayed.

The Lord suffered all for me,
the debt He freely paid.

I feel grateful yet for such a chance,
to serve with all my soul.

The snow is deep yet I will pay,
this small and simple toll.

Groves in the wood fit perfectly,
my fingers now so thin.

Each morning, I kneel down to pray,
and I push along within.

I lay each child in their grave,
so peaceful and so still.

I sing to God with all my strength,
I praise Him in this winter chill.

Quietly and slowly,
I grind my humble food.

My belly filled up with His word,
I read that He is good.

I pray that those who follow,
find me where I lay.

Unable to go on,
no longer able to obey.

So peaceful and so calm,
I lie in wait to go.

My savior's arms then comfort me,
I still must reap, I still must sow.

My feet now worn down to the bone,
a red trail I leave behind.

My brother suffered more than I,
His face clear in my mind.

Frigid air then coils around my face,
freezing like a stone.

I cannot see who pushes me,
I hope I am not alone.

My eyes heavy with fatigue,
the frost so cold I bleed.

A blazing fire then cleaves my heart,
and my eyes are clear to see.

A valley bright with snow,
and I know that I am home.

My savior leads me forward,
I know I am not alone.

Repentance

My savior and redeemer,
I have great need of thee.

It cannot wait much longer,
I wish I would be free.
My needs are great this evening,
I come now unto thee.

Have mercy on this sinner,
help a man lost in his way.
Show me back to the path that,
leads to my Father's house.

Where the streets are paved with light,
a place where everything is sweet.

Give me rest for all tomorrow,
please I need to show retreat.

The enemy is gaining,
I need thee now to beat,
that great and terrible dragon,
that never ceases to be seen.

I need thy guidance through,
this turbulence and sleet.

I cannot hold much longer,
I am small and frail and weak.

I call thee to my side tonight,
let me fight upon thy right.

I have need of thy grace,
grateful is my heart to thee.

The payment has long been made,
comforting my weak heart.

My Lord, I stand before Thy throne,
before the judgment seat.

My garments pure and white,
I remember no wrongdoings done.

While testing in thy sight,
many times I felt to flee.

I will now progress on forward,
and with Thee I know I am free.

Turn

I come to a wall, one I cannot scale,
I cannot break.

I spend my time staring up and up,
with no end in sight.

To avoid it I do all I can,
I do not want this here to stand.

I speak to myself,
as though to reason.

There must be a way,
around, over,
or beneath.

But no matter how I search,
I cannot see a way.

So I simply sit,
and try to forget that the wall is even there.

It's so ugly and obtrusive,
I cannot look away.

I feel so beaten and so betrayed,
by this path I was told to take.

Walls before have been in my way,
but nothing such as this.

I have a follower on my path,
but I have never paid Him heed.

Always there and always silent,
but never to be missed.

He stays right on my path,
as though He cannot find another.

Perhaps He is not strong enough,
to go on a path of His own.

He does not speak,
could he be waiting for me?

I do all I can to ignore Him too,
and get on with my way.

I do more and more to fight this wall,
to beat it and prove my strength.

More hopeless and degrading,
no man can cross this wall.

I bury my pride and I sink in deep,
and I turn to face this Man.

One who has watched me and seen my struggle,
yet not a finger does He lift.

I walk to Him and seek His help,
to find my way through.

He gladly helps, gives me His advice,
though insane He sounds to me.

"Walk through the wall, don't run or jump,
and you will make it safely there."

"I will help you and guide your way,
though you may stumble, and you may break."

"Together we will make it through,
fear not that you may fall."

I follow Him, though doubtingly,
I have no other way.

Together we gently touch the wall,
and my fingers slip right through.

I thank the Man for His help,
and he smiles and says cheerfully.

I will always be here with you,
all you need to do is turn.

Wait

I call unto my God,
yet no answer do I hear.

Has my Lord forgotten,
has He failed to know my prayer?

Humbly, I kneel down to Him,
and yet no answer appears.

Perhaps I have fallen short,
committed some type of error.

I was taught in church and Sunday school,
to kneel and ask on high.

They told me He would answer me,
yet it seems He is not there.

They told me that He loved me,
yet I feel not Him near or nigh.

Why can't He answer my request?
Does He truly not even care?

So many others have testified,
that God has spoken aloud.

If He can speak to those who sin,
why can't he speak to me?

I do my best to seek the good,
have I been jealous or maybe proud?

Why can't He open my eyes to glory,
so that I may finally see?

My scriptures lie flat on my desk,
He has planted His small seed.

My eyes draw near to the book I loved,
and I lose all of my cares.

My Lord is there and watching me,
I know as I read.

In My time and in My way,
I shall answer all that thou may need.

Why Would He Care for Me?

Why would God care for me,
a tiny human being?

I'm nothing compared to those on high,
I'm weak and frail in heart.

Why would a being as He,
care so much for me?

His power is unending,
His miracles never seem to cease.

He used so many men in time,
to carry on His work.

With Moses He freed Israel,
with him He split the sea.

With Noah He saved all that breathed,
with him He cleansed the Earth.

With Enoch He moved mountains,
with him He made a perfect nation.

With Daniel He gave a lion's courage,
with him He gave a dream.

With Nephi He gave spirit and strength,
with him He taught the truth.

With Moroni He gave such great faith,
with him He set the standard.

With Joseph He restored His truth,
with him He showed the way.

But I am nothing compared to these,
I cannot stand with such great men.
Why would He care for me?

I have no great accomplishments,
I have tamed no lioness.

I have done no more to glory God,
than to stand as a witness for Him.

He has so many on this day,
why would He want one more?

The Being who controls the Earth and stars,
why would He answer me?

The answer is simple,
yet not many know.

I am His child,
and I love Him.

Such a simple answer,
for why He cares for me.

The Fire Within

The torch has been lit,
the fight has begun.

The battle in darkness,
with horror and sin.

Sparks flying skyward,
ignite my still heart.

The enemy deceives,
with no mercy he strikes.

The quickening scorch,
saves those trapped in the dark.

As I light those around me,
I see all in need.

This ember I hold,
growing strong in its time.

My fire then bursts,
the darkness engulfed.

No hope for my foe,
no more sorrow or sin.

It's time to refine,
the fire within!

Man

Man begotten from the earth,
Woman of his bone.

All the world at their domain,
yet something they did lack.

Innocent and clean,
they did care for all around.

No joy did they find,
nor happiness, nor sin.

Obedient for sure,
Eternal and faithful.

They followed God's commandment,
no more, no less.

Perfect was the state of life,
with no hope and no regret.

A slithering and slimy thing,
to disrupt and destroy.

Deception and beguiling follow,
before this foul cold thing.

A commandment broken,
joyous triumph from the ground.

Foiled yet was this creature,
this people began the way.

For a disciple will not be made,
if sin has not knocked upon the door.

Let Him Ask of God

Words of mercy from the Savior,
fill my heart with peace and joy.

How can I see once again,
through the eyes of those who've gone before?

The thought of His great payment,
makes me tremble in my state.

Though I know I am a sinner,
I need to find the true right way.

How can I find that pearl of knowledge,
one that seemed to slip away.

Many have come to profess the word,
yet I do not feel Him there.

They preach their doctrine so differently,
how could I know the truth?

Perplexed by those who try to lead,
those that think they know what's real.

In the Bible I find the answer,
in the holy word of God.

James then gives me all I sought,
I must go and ask in faith.

In a grove I seek for answers,
beneath the trees I bow.

A creeping darkness then constrains me,
seizing upon my very being.

Showing absolutely no restraint,
my soul begins to break.

Dragged down to Hell, my mind then searing,
my heart convulsed and straining.

With what little strength I have,
I mutter a single, simple prayer.

A light then wraps around my sight,
a pillar from above the sky.

Peace flows in to ignite my soul,
a flame which cannot scorch.

What my eyes beheld I cannot doubt,
I know what I have seen.

Fear then returns as two Men descend,
surely to make an end.

Yet I hear my name and fear no longer,
as I behold The Father and His Son.

I Remember Him

Two boys have knocked upon my door,
they say they are sent by God.

Surely there is no such thing as this,
no great and mighty One.

They say they have good news to share,
they ask for a little time.

Time is one thing I cannot spare,
but yet I feel I should.

They speak of Christ and suffering,
of salvation and of family.

They ask to come into my home,
to teach and testify.

Though timid and unsure,
I open my door and I step aside.

They tell me of great and marvelous things,
I cannot help but believe.

They ask me to follow Christ's example,
to be cleansed of all my sins.

My heart then bursts into open flames,
I cannot doubt the truth.

I remember now before this life,
the faith I once possessed.

I knew my savior and I worshiped Him,
He told me of this life and trials.

Yet I accepted the call to come to Earth,
to fight and to win.

I answer them amidst tears of joy,
I will surely follow once again.
For I remember Him.

A Babe of Glory

A babe of glory,
now born to Earth.

Shepherds leading flocks abroad,
at an angel's biding hand.

Three men chosen gather near,
prepared to witness this day.

Angels of the heavens rejoice,
glorious triumph they now see.

Trumpets from on high to blaze,
souls waiting to be saved.

Fragile in His mother's arms,
delicate and small.

Strength emanating from this God,
forever pure and clean.

Salvation comes of this young babe,
delivery beginning with His name.

Men of Israel now long past,
sang praises of this day.

Dust rising to His name,
shining brightly into the haze.

Soldiers then prepared to fight,
faithfully waiting to be called.

His troops now armed,
His captains awaiting the sound.

Sentinels now standing by,
called to guard and protect.

I witnessed this day from up above,
from the home I seek to find once more.

Soldier I was called and soldier I now am,
called to serve Him of humble birth.

Willing to come down to Earth,
Jehovah begins His reign!

Refiners Fire

My savior chose me,
in the direst of times was I called.

To prepare for the future,
for what He had in store.

Though fallen and weak,
He asked me to survive.

To lead and to guide,
to show others the way.

Through the inferno of affliction,
I have risen and renewed.

Through the pain of refinement,
I returned into His ranks.

Purified by His fire,
I now lead and I fight.

Burned of all blemish and sin,
I defend at His front line.

Faced with all affliction,
sends me inches from the veil.

Hated of all men,
for the name upon my chest.

A dragon's breath seeks to destroy,
yet it cannot scorch or burn.

Willing to step into the heart of the heat,
I will choose to proceed and live.

I will not forsake,
I will step in stride.

Walking through the valley,
the shadow of death with Thee.

Peter

Called to gather and forsake,
I come at just His word.

I followed the Lord out onto the deep,
yet from fear, I do sink and drown.

I was given power,
that all under my hand may last.

Like the King I must forgive,
I must never forsake.

I witness the suffering for all,
my eyes heavy and strained.

Thrice I deny,
bitter are my tears.

Never again will I forsake,
I will witness till the end.

Bringing salvation to those once unclean,
showing all the way.

Thomas

Distress fills my heart,
tears flow free as I observe.

My friend and my teacher,
hung upon a tree.

I return to my home,
depressed and confused.

Why would He come just to die,
just to let foul men defile?

Three days now past in mourning,
grief-stricken and disdained.

Word comes of life,
of the Masters rising they claim.

Doubt fills my heart,
how could this truly be?

I must see and I must feel,
or I will not believe.

Jesus comes with shut doors,
in glory does He appear.

My feeble hands reach forth,
at His beckon I feel.

Trembling I fall to my knees,
humbled I manage to whisper.

My Lord and my God... I believe.

My Storm

My life is hard,
I cannot continue on.

The grief I feel,
the terror in my heart.

I have no choice,
I accept my fate.

I search my mind,
for another way.

There is but one,
He could help.

He could save my life,
yet all He does is sleep.

Why don't You care?
Why do You slumber?

Can You not see,
the storm before?

He wakes His eyes,
and begins to speak.

"You do not know what is to come,
the future holds a raging storm."

"One you alone cannot survive,
have faith in me and do not doubt."

"If you only seek,
I will calm the clouds."

"Do what I ask,
I will cast away your fears."

Beyond the Veil

I cannot see behind this world,
I cannot get beneath it.

I cannot seem to stretch the fabric,
nor can I even reach it.

I know it's there,
for I have seen a glimpse between it.

I know not how,
but I know I can recede it.

I've heard of men,
who have rarely seen beyond it.

I have been told,
there are many just beside it.

I know it's there,
I truly do believe it.

Even though,
I have yet to truly see it.

Death Has No Sting

His hands broken,
His feet torn and frayed.

To suffer for the weak,
the lost and forgotten.

Through trial and pain,
He suffered unto death.

To save the putrid,
the vile and obsessed.

A stone wedged firm,
Guards set in place.

To protect the proud,
to futile grace.

Three days decay,
stench turns to rot.

Ignorant souls redeemed,
subject and taught.

Dregs now drunk,
His angels venture near.

Set free the Light,
to take captive fear.

The debt was paid
the King of Kings reigns.

For a new week is born,
and the angels shout.

He is not here,
He is risen.

For behold today,
He lives!

The Last Draft

Enlistment entices on either side,
I find myself unsure.

But which is best I must decide,
there is no neutral ground.

Recruiters approach at every angle,
all trying to persuade and guide.

From this war I cannot hide,
I cannot run away.

Both promise of great things to come,
one of happiness, one of pain.

A whisper slips into my mind,
a voice both great and calm.

Assured and unafraid I choose,
With confidence I enroll.

Unfazed I march toward battle,
the front line of this great war.

Ready I stand, prepared to fight,
Unwavering I plant my feet.

Scarred and bruised I hold my place.
yet too many give up and fall.

Though hopeless seems our victory,
The Savior is on our side.

We decide to follow Him,
or give up the fight and die.

It's my choice if I survive,
I choose to live or die.

How to Grow a Tree

A tree grows not by impatience or demand,
it cannot flourish smothered by shadow.

First the earth must be broken,
fertile, pliable, and soft.

A good seed planted in the best of ground,
the best plot of land.

Nurture must follow,
if this seed is to grow.

Time and attention is needed,
or it may not even sprout.

Exposure to the Son is key,
living water must be a priority.

Constant watch you must retain,
that fowls do not devour and take.

Through hard work and labor,
this tree will take root.

This time and this effort,
will strengthen this seed.

One day it will grow,
its branches spread out.

More seeds will then follow,
for others to grow.

All this was done because you took the time,
to read the book on how to plant a tree.

White Is the Field, Great Is the Harvest

A sickle slipping in my hand,
blistered, beaten, torn.

Harvest time is almost through,
life seeming to wear thin.

I cannot stop to rest a bit,
for the field has been matured.

The grain is ready to be cut,
almost asking me to swing.

Enduring heat of the day,
the seed will not waist.

I serve with many loyal men,
yet some give up and quit.

Those who stay lay up in store,
the blessings as his pay.

Hard it is to keep my strength,
I have need to be sustained.

Often I fall down to my knees,
humbled, my weak heart shown.

He knows my struggle and fatigue,
He gives me water in desperate need.

The day has ended, my job is done,
It's time to journey home.

I walk through gates, tired and worn,
but with vigor I venture through.

Peace settles into my mind,
as I think it's time to rest.

But when I behold the other side,
I see yet another crop.

For the field is white,
and ready to harvest.

So I will wear upon my chest forever,
The King of Kings, His crest.

Atlas

Father take this from upon my back,
this load so hard to bear.

I cannot hold much longer,
I must break down and share.

I have done all that I can,
pride stripped and bare.

Take what I cannot control,
hold what I do not dare.

My shoulders now weak,
deliver me from all care.

Help me in my struggle,
untangle me from this snare.

Powerless I now see I am,
Thy Son crushed with none to compare.

Slothful and content with man,
Lifting myself in the air.

Arrogance controlled my heart,
I see why people stare.

The guilt inside so eager,
to mold into a nightmare.

Redeem me from my punishment,
remove me from this glare.

Take this world from my back,
hear my pleading prayer.

Atoning Blood

Pain so soft,
beats through my heart.
The liquid of my death gives life,
to body and to soul.

Great puddles form beneath my knees,
I cannot stop this fall.
A pleading prayer for it to stop,
my will is not my own.

Tears of red stream out of skin,
like an olive in a press.
The air of life comes hard to me,
I wish it to pass over.

My clothes now scarlet,
yet I am white as snow.
The crimson stains across my face,
what once was white like wool.

One more soul to save,
The pain will ever grow.
My body through all pain,
all hope.

The Joy of My suffering,
to bring My grace to just one soul.
To save him from his sins,
that he may be free.

If I was meant to save just one,
I would rejoice with him.
All have the chance to accept,
my blood torn soaking robe.

In grace and mercy I will come,
for those who shared My pain.
Come to me in thine hour,
and I will succor thee.

Choose

I can be mean,
filled in vile obsess.

Putrid in nature,
content with death.

My ego bulging,
bloated in distress.

Pride streaking my veins,
constricting my best breath.

I can be kind,
turn the other cheek.

Love my neighbor,
help in all I can.

Show pure charity,
guiding poor who seek.

Walk close with virtue,
to a path I cannot plan.

I am all these things,
and these things are me.

It's up to me what I will be,
I decide what I can see.

Yet what truly matters,
is what I choose to be.

Listen

Man is not worthy,
he is lower than the dust.

He seeks to satisfy,
the devil from within.

Impurity and sin,
a desire from below.

Man's ear cannot be sanctified,
to digest words from above.

Yet, God speaks,
His voice comes subtly.

To anyone who may listen,
ears open to His voice.

God's word will spread,
for he speaks the truth.

We do not deserve the word,
yet He wants us all to hear.

Let us pray to seek His word,
and ask Him what is true.

I have one question,
before we start.

What will you do when he speaks,
when He calls for you?

Change

I am moved in my mind,
to act on my heart.

These things shown to me,
could not truly be.

Why do I desire,
what I choose not to believe?

A notion pressed upon,
my body and soul.

My Father has spoken,
truths unto my ear.

What is false is removed,
truth willingly endures.

Why won't this thought fade,
how can I escape?

Unwillingly I feel,
a pulse in my heart.

This truth is beyond,
what I can explain.

I give up my heart,
I give back my soul.

To the Creator of life,
the answer to death.

The goodness of God,
the defeater of sin.

CPSIA information can be obtained
at www.ICGtesting.com
Printed in the USA
LVHW050745080323
741126LV00005B/847

9 781643 785479